SZNs of Love
by
Rolanda Sue

A note from the author

Hey friends, thank you for supporting my dreams as an
author and for supporting this first book of mine.
This book is a collection of poems that tell one love
story.
You will see this love develop and change as the
seasons change. As you read you will think of those
people who you have experienced love with
and I hope that this
serves as a way to release that old thing and jump
into something new. I wholeheartedly love this
collection of poems and I hope you do as well.

I love interaction so I want you to use this
collection as inspiration to create. As you read this
book feel free to design your own cover art for
poems, mark it up with words or thoughts, create your
own poems of love, create music, clothing,
whatever your thing is, CREATE.
I would love to see where your thoughts, feelings
and imagination takes you,
so as you create share them with me.
IG: @ro.suee or FB: @ro.sueee.

I loosely 'suggest' reading this collection in one
sitting &
as you read press play on
J. Bosco - Butterflies in the Winter Album
found on Apple Music & Spotify.

Poetry is ..

You dont know I wrote
this, but... you're
teaching me to
love & trust,
ms. Sue!
1-8-15

Table of Contents

What's Love?

What's love anyway?
A word, a thought, a feeling, an action?

is it just a mere word that I utter
to be on one accord with another
is it just a thought of sweet songs and butterfly
tummies
maybe a feeling so deep that neither words nor feelings
can be used to express the tingling feelings within
or maybe love is neither of those things,
maybe love is an action.
Love a verb.
A verb that represents doing instead of saying,
doing instead of thinking,
doing instead of feeling...a verb..an action.
The act of putting others before yourself
The act of respect
The act of happiness and joy
The act of not judging
The act of embracing others that aren't like you
The act of trusting on a man's word
The act of forgiveness, mercy, and grace.
Love ..a verb..an action.
I may not know for sure
but one thing I do know is that love is within us all.
God spoke to himself when he created us.
He spoke to HIMSELF ..the ultimate source of LOVE.
GOD is LOVE.
We are made in his likeness and image so we are love.
Unleash your God potential of love and spread it
whether it is a word, a thought, a feeling
or an action.
What's love?

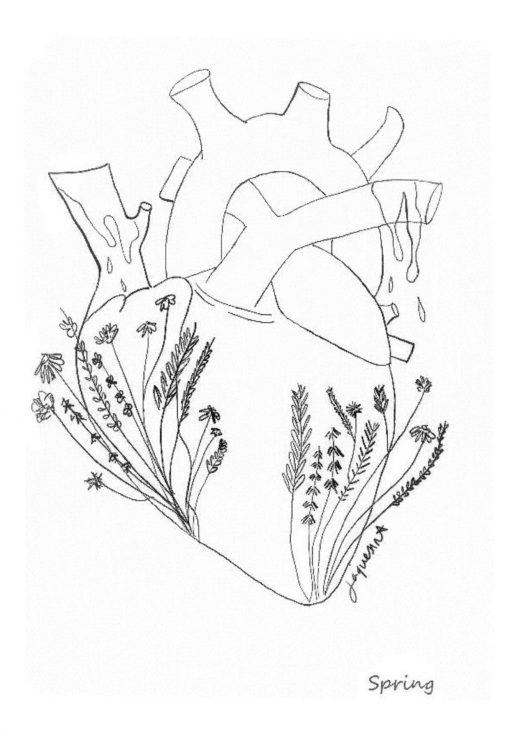

Spring

rolanda

author • speaker • p
rolandasue@gmail.c

linkedin: rolanda sue • facebook: @
twitter: @ro.suee • author ig: @experienc

Winter

Sometimes it's hard to smile
when all I feel like doing is crying
No shoulder to lean on
so my pillow cases I weep on
No ear to voice my concerns
so my pad I write on
No one to relate to my pain
so I bottle and lock the cap
Strong exterior, tough walls
silent cries, she suffers
Lonely nights as she slumbers
lonely heart as she wonders
will she find someone that will compliment her
It's a scary thought that she may never know
the feeling of being in love
because she placed her heart
in a cement block a long time ago
Knock, knock, guys keep knocking
but all seem to be using the wrong tools
to break the cement block she guards like a warden

She lays and wonders
whatever happened to getting that old thing back
the past always seems to trigger those old memories
And who is new when everyone is old
and every girl has taken a toll on his heart
leaving anyone new just as another wounded soul
She seems hopeless in this cold world
cold walls , cold minds, cold thoughts
hopelessly yearning for love
But how can she emulate something that is foreign to her
no father mother relationship
that could draw a blueprint for her
So I guess she'll just continue to smile
Even when she feels like crying
with no shoulder to lean on
only her pillows cases to weep on

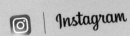

Instagram

@ro.suee

Follow me on Instagram for a daily dose of poetry, inspiration, devotionals and much more! #sznsofro

Lost

Footprints in the sand
but her feet refuse to follow them
Road maps with highlighted highways
but her eyes can't see them
GPS with voice directions
but her ears are deaf to them
All possible guides
but her next self won't let her follow them
Why is it that she is stuck in the same place
when all the directions have been spelled out?
She refuses to give any options a try
So she sits at a green light
looking left and right
remains sitting
Go ahead and drive
The unknown may be what she needs to grow
She keeps walking
hand full of directions but refers to none
Decides that she'd rather be lost
than repeat paths taken before
So she gathers her things
and thread in her own direction
tosses maps and began to create
her own footprints in the sand

Dreams

You visit me every night in my dreams
but I don't recognize your face,
when will you reveal yourself to me in your entity??
maybe you're here to tease me of what could be,
but why play such a cruel joke on poor me.
I wake up wishing that these dreams will be my
reality
only to be disappointed with no you and still only
just me.
I would be a better person with you right next to me
but I think I get your true quest for my destiny.
Until you reveal yourself I won't sleep.
My journey will continue in trying to better me.
Until that goal is ultimately reached
only then will I consider sleep
maybe then I'll reach my full potential
and what you expect of me
and I've come to the conclusion
that only then I'd want you to reveal your image to
me,
making a perfect match of what should be.
Just you and me ultimately creating one entity
until that day I vow to do right by me
in hopes that I'll be good enough
for your unmasking ceremony
showing your true persona and
not just what I assume you to be
No rush needed, I'll wait patiently
to see what's in store for me
I guess time is the key that reveals you to me

Friend

I need a friend
Not a foe
Not someone that's just going to go along with the
flow
Not someone that's going to leech from the fountain
Not someone that's just in it to take
But rather ..
A friend
One that's going to hold me accountable
One that's going to share my soul
Connections that only come in the spirit
I need a friend
One that's going to check me when I'm wrong
One that's going to drive to the end of the world
I need a friend
One that's not going to leave me for dead
Or strip me of myself
A friend
I need a friend

Scars

Cut deep as a child
Left lost searching for love
Sometimes in all the wrong places
Sometimes in all the right ones
Unknowingly when he left
He took a massive piece of me
Leaving a cut that eventually healed
But left me with a scar
To remember him
So every time I glanced at my heart
I see that it was broken
Never to be pristine again
Because the scar has so much meaning
Feelings of loneliness and pain
Feelings of abandonment and neglect
Half stepping in all relationships
Always aware that this scar can be repeated
Only thing this time I'd have a part in it
Maybe another scar is needed
To grow me emotionally
Because this time I'll know that I
Controlled half of the piercing
But for now I'll let this scar
Be a reminder for two reasons
It was never your fault that he left
Don't leave scars that resemble the one on your chest
For you're better than he'll ever be
Continue to be the light of love unconditionally
And always remember that no matter how you're treated
Never leave scars
Because although they will heal
Those hurts will always remain

Black

Is the color of your melanin filled skin
& as the sun hits I can't forget how it glistened
BLACK
Like the identity you are
Never allowed yourself to be
Buried by mans self righteousness
BLACK
You were the epitome of power and love
And when my eyes connected with yours
It was a clash of cultures,
Waves of buried heritage revealed with every blink
BLACK
Decades of hurt but when we met
It was as if all the pain became shackled
& all the sweetness of your being
was finally recognized
All the pain finally reconciled
BLACK - 'ER'
the berry, sweeter the juice
& your juice became the sweetest taste to my lips
BLACK
The ambition couldn't be buried
You were that rose that grew without being water
You bloomed from soil unfertilized
BLACK
Your presence is commanding, covering all space
With hope & love
Bleeding truth, watering your own seeds of love
BLACK
You became the sunlight that my heart
Needed to bloom
You became the flowers after every moon
You became the heartbeat & quickly my favorite tune
BLACK
You became love in its truest form
BLACK
You became light I needed to see
BLACK
You became the favorite parts of me

Eyes

The gateway to the soul
The opening to a hello
The pain behind a goodbye
The look given when you're in love
The magic of the first time
The eyes
The gateway to life
Always willing to tell your story
Even when your mouth refuses to move
Always snitching behind every feeling
My eyes share the glare
Of love when it glances at you
Glistens with blossoming flowers
And breezy palm trees
Of sunsets
And waves on my feet
Trust these eyes
as they fall so slowly
In love with you

Under Construction

When you met me
I was a work of art
Not too complex
Not too basic
Not too deep
Not too bleak
It was spring
I knew you would be special
Simply by the way
You said my name
With just enough love
And a lot of bliss
You became my favorite
You watered my soul
And I allowed it to bloom
I was a work of art
Under construction
Abstract
But you filled my rigged
Black lines with color
You poured joy into my life
Your hands became
The tools needed
To mend this broken heart

Bloom

The trees were beginning to bloom
And so was this new love
The pink and white
Flowers began to flourish
The drops of rain
Watered our love
Watered our hearts

Your timing was perfect
Our love grew with every sunrise
And simmered with every sunset

You made me fall
For the sweet smell of flowers
And fresh cut grass
Spring became my favorite season
You became the flower
That bloomed
In my cement heart

Love Better

Yes better
cause in the past
Worst was what I called my best
And feelings had no home
In this chest
But when I met you
Well ..
you defied the laws of physics I was used to
Instead of following my usual
Path of destruction
You showed me how to follow you
Like Newton said, I was in motion
No longer in rest
Because you were the force
That gave me life
Changed the course of my definition of love
Because with you better is what I dreamed of
And instead of running from the law
I became a law abiding citizen
And although sometimes I struggle with this force
That seems to change my course of broken records
I find myself becoming less and less
Of the rebel
That would commit the crime and run
Snatch a soul
And watch it drown in its sorrows
Just to evade the hurt
That I always thought would come
But you ..
You make me want to love better
Not just for the sake of keeping you around
But so that I can make myself proud
To finally say I let the facade down
You ..
You make me want to love better

Run forest run

Run forest run
Seems like the older I get the faster I run
Farther away from the dream of happiness I phantom
Feeling as if I don't deserve this one
Another set up like the first one

But I don't even give a fight to change the course
Similar to the hamster on his wheel
Hops on everyday thinking of a new dream
Thinking this time I'll make it out the cage
Not realizing it's a controlled circle
that shapes' never change

But I realize it's a weakness
So here is my first step I call it admittance.
Time to quit running like the first one
Stop forest, stop the run
Fight for the happiness
You deserve this one

Peace

Where water meets feet
And sand meets toes
And sunlight meets skin
Dipped in a calming presence
Of nostalgia
Surrounded by nature's own
God's creations
Unique in every special way
Waves crashing against the shore
Trees swaying with the wind
Immersed in the comforter of love
A sense of certainty
All while igniting
The imagination around the unknown
Unable to see what the future holds
Yet standing firmly in this peace
Of right now
Still
Unwavering
Strong
Peace

Yellow

You brought color to my life
But yellow was the
Color I thought of
When I thought of you
You shined bright
Like the sunlight
And your smile
Lit up my life
I never knew
You could be so sweet
Like honey in my tea
Yellow
Was the color
That I thought of
When I thought of you

Tender Love

Before you
I didn't know
This touch
You were gentle
You were soft
You were tender
I didn't know
Man could be like
Flowers that bloomed
I didn't know
That man could be so sweet
I didn't know
That man could be so soft
But you defied
What I thought I knew
You were the
Expression of peace
And the sweet visual
Of new spring leaves
You became this
Tender love
I never knew could exist
You became
My bliss
Everything a girl
Could wish

Safe place to be weak

I got trapped in this family
of dysfunction and pain
caused from long time heartache
and different mental states
I didn't know if father would
be coming or going
he was trapped by his mental state
forced to grow up at the age of 8
a little adult
who could tell me anything?
food needed, I cooked it
clothes needed, I washed it
bedtime reached, I set it
my life was a mimic
of what I saw
everything I did was to mirror the images
that were played by the picture perfect
actors on stages
routines became familiar
lies became my truth
and pain was the fuel
to be PERFECT
so that I wouldn't end up like mama
PERFECT
so no one would notice the neglect
PERFECT
so that no one would visit
but all the while I was being eaten up inside
dark thoughts of suicide
endless crying and sleepless nights
all awhile I just felt trapped
always searching for that
safe place that I could be free,
you became that safe place I could be weak

Interlude -- #Dreams

Dreams   06/03/15

Flowers resonate from leafless winter trees
Blossoming from warm air and spring breeze
Is this what love feels like when it's no longer
a dream
Seeds growing into trees that can withstand
any speed
Of winds that move
clouds floating high above the sky
as your smile seems to gleam and
you take me to cloud 9

Is this love really true?
Are the feelings that I feel for you & only you
Is my task to pick you up when you
down & feeling blue?
Or is my job to tell you that I love you

Roosters sound as the sunrise
waking me up to glare in your eyes
through the meadows at long eye lashes
how long will the fairytale of this dream last
Its to real to be true
So I pinch myself to make sure its you
and that im the lucky one that has you
So I ask....

Is this love really true?
Are the feeling that I feel for you & only you
Is my task to pick you up when you down
and feeling blue?
Or is my job to tell you that I love you

#Dreams

44

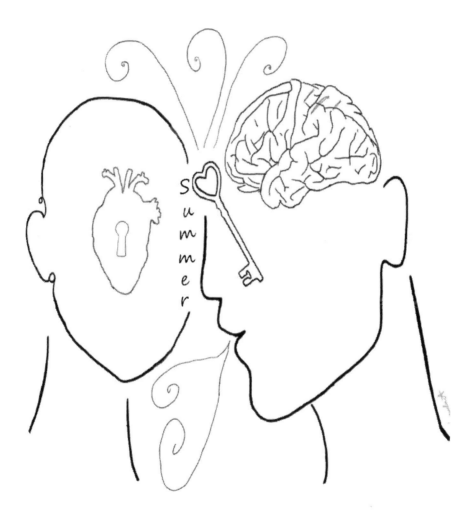

Red lips

Stained in every crevice
Plumped
Just patiently waiting
For a kiss
Leave a mark on your neck
Having your friends
Inquiring
Whose red lips?

LBD

Yes the one she pulls out on special occasions
The ultimate thirst trap
Hugs every curve smoothly
No room to breathe
Or for panties
Kissing every crease in her skin
The little black dress
She kept just for you
To notice her sexy
Without her having to say a thing
Or make a move

Drifting on you

That's all I can do when I look at you
Have to catch myself cause
I'm always drifting on blue
Or should I say drifting on you
Dazed blue oceans that glisten
When sunlight hit its core

& you may not know this but when
I'm with you your eyes remind me
Of the passion of crashing waves
As the ocean roars

It's like I'm the light your lenses needed to see
or maybe I'm just over zealous
in my description of me

Either way infinity is what I see
when I'm looking into your eyes
drifting on blue
Or should I say drifting on you

One day

One day we'll have a son
And we'll name him after a king
Teach him about Jesus
And some other faithful men
Teach him how to love himself
And how to be fearless
Teach him that courage comes by practice
And patience with grace
Teach him it's okay to cry
And share how he feels
Teach him how to practice compassion
Even when he fears
Teach him the importance of his story
And the power of a testimony
Teach him he is chosen
And only God gets the glory
One day we'll have a son
And we'll name him after a King
We'll teach him to be like you
Tender -- hearted
One day
We'll have a sun

Fireworks

Light it up
BOOM
Fire away
She thought
Started so subtly
Just add heat
Slow spark
It's a shoota
Hits the sky
Adds light
To the dark night
Only for a moment
In the dark night
An eruption
So bright
Then back
To square one
No light
Light it up
BOOM

Open

Open up to me,
vulnerably
let me keep your secrets
hide your words
in my thoughts
capture your tears
in my bosom
open up to me,
vulnerably
trust me with your truths
& give me a chance to
choose you
every version of you
consistently
open up to me,
vulnerably
let me heal
all the parts of you
you don't want anyone to see
let me pour love
In every broken piece of you
we'd call it art
a beautiful creation
of what was
& what's about to be

Thirst

Trapping since the 90s
Tried to be subtle with the drizzle
But shawty bad, No effort
Or shawty, tryna make up
For something that happened in the past
So she sends half naked pictures
To grab your attention
Attention needing to be quenched
Toxic coming in and going out
Thirsty so you drank from the well
For it was polluted water
She poured from within
Touched by a man at a young age
So her prerogative is to expose her skin
Because she thinks she deserved it
So here she is half naked
Thirst trapping men with every social media flick
And they drink
From poisoned water to quench their lustful thirst
Looks like it was a setup on both ends
She been trapping since tainted
And he's been keeping his mouth wet
With every tainted sip

All of You

Exactly as you are
No tweaks
No changes
Unless made by the almighty
I won't let you do anything unorthodox
Except love me with your whole self
I know I'm sounding a bit selfish
But excuse the
Territorial issues
That kick in overdrive
When it comes to you
Never wanting you gone
Afraid you'll never return
Just like the one that broke my heart
But if you're not ready
For such a responsibility
Let me know
Cause I want all of you
Not just pieces
That don't link
To make us complete
All of you
24/7

Last night

Last night
I needed you
Or should I say I wanted you bad
A whiff of your scent on my sheets
was what I was missing
Warmth that drew me in
as I slumbered until morning
Last night I wanted you bad
Big hands as they rubbed across my thighs
Sweet soft kisses as it tickled down my spine
And my body squirm cause
of the attraction those lips create
when they attach to my skin
Last night I wanted you bad
Head rubs and back rubs as you slumbered
Cold nights, comfy pillows and comforters
Entangled in our space
As I drag my leg across your thigh
and get all up in your space
Last night I wanted you bad
But I couldn't stomach the courage
to ask if I could get a whiff
of that scent on my sheets
with a sprinkle of those
sweet kisses on my cheeks
Last night I wanted you bad

Addicted to Your Love

I'm addicted to your love
I'm addicted to your love
A curse?
A blessing?
You accept me
My light and shadow
You make me feel safe
You teach me about myself
You include me in your life
You keep me humble
You let me invade your space
You take care of me
Your eyes pierce my soul
You're not predictable
You're always warm when I'm cold
You always let me wear your clothes
You smell like fresh showers and starry skies
You remind me you miss me with kisses
You grip me tight when I'm acting shy
I'm addicted to YOU love
I'm addicted to YOU love
A curse?
A blessing?

Organ in Her Chest

This beating organ in her chest
Got caught slipping, or should I say skipping
Beats that beat for you
Your touch , Your smell, Your taste
Is what it longs for
To know if this love thing is real ..Yes real
Because you appealed to the organ in her chest
Right between her breast
And instead of thinking of the mess
She connects to the musical beats
Feeling in unchartered territory
Cause normally she feels with her brain;
Logistically
Rehashing all the past contingencies
Making love seem like a fantasy
Rather a fairytale only seen in a Disney movie
For years the organ in her head
Overpowered that in her chest
Easy to disconnect from any mess
Brain vs. heart
Somehow the brain would always win
Able to always recollect all the memories
The heart would forget
Yet with you
The heart seems to overpower
The organ in her head
overpowered by over feeling
And not over analysis
And although the heart has been strong for so long
So many walls continue to fall
I just hope heart knows what she's doing
Because if heartbreak comes from this feeling of bliss
I'm afraid she'll get stuck in her old cycle of brain
analysis
Afraid to feel with the organ in her chest
But instead fall victim to the memories of pain and hurt
From recollected thoughts produced
By the organ in her head

Broken hearted cry

He whispers sweet nothings in her ear as she walks by
He thinks this will heal her broken hearted cry
He tries to swindle his way within her open mind
trying to plant the seed about a better life

He's persistent so he tries to court her
tries to make moves that will benefit her
tries to show he cares by cooking for her
He runs a bath
massages her
pampers her
and treats her like a queen
He cries out
my queen my queen
let me into your kingdom your majesty

He looks to her for an answer
only to notice that all his actions had gone
unnoticed
If only she had looked into his eyes
she would have seen the sincerity of his intent
but she was so blinded by the darkness
of past kings that did her wrong
It was then that he realized
that his queen was deaf
From her own broken hearted cry

Remember

We're drifting like objects in a sea
Been under attack by heavy waves
Clashing against our bodies
Trying to stay afloat in this
Relationship game
But seems like
I'm the only one trying
To stay afloat
I look up
You've drifted farther away
But
I just ask
That you fight the currents
Weather the storm
REMEMBER
All the sunny summer days
All the memories captured
All the laughs shared
All the happiness
All the heartbeats felt
REMEMBER
Every time your lips touched mine
Every touch that felt so right
REMEMBER
All the times that made us
Those that shifted us and brought us closer
Hold on to the life jacket
I'm here to help you swim instead of sink
Let's add this to the list of things
We can remember
About how we weathered the storm together

Truth

Fact or fiction
Gimme facts
I'd rather live with which I can't change
Than piece together narratives of tales
Gimme facts
Let me heart check you
Test your trust in me with your truth
Gimme facts
Let me guard my own emotions
Don't make decisions for me
Gimme facts
So I won't have to wonder
About anything else you've said
Gimme facts
For its always better than fiction

Beauty in her pain

There was always beauty in her pain
Hurt in her eyes
Lies in her smile
But she presented a force like a flood
Love came rushing in with every encounter of her
She made you feel exhilarating
And filled you with bliss
But on the inside she was hurting
Battling with decisions made
And opportunities missed
Love lost
And words not spoken
She knew exactly how to make you feel wanted
Created experiences she never felt
Attempting to fill a void with all the wrong things
There was always beauty in her pain
Hurt in her eyes
Lies in her smile
And even though she struggled with the pain
Her beauty came from the love she always shared

Interlude -- #Goodbye

#GOODBYE

God lee, I'm leaving on bad terms,
but I'ma only be gone for the season of germs,
You'll understand my reason when I come back overseas
and you see the stacks I earned,
I promise you gon' get that salary back without
the salary cap like a tax return,
Just think, five years from now,
we'll be dressed down, just mink,
call the family down for the babyshower, Just pink
Guess what? we're havin a daughter,
Let's elope and think of all the pretty names we
could call her, next let's shoot for a baller,
I'ma pave the way so one day he'll be as great as
his father,
Now you're only 30 years young and get to live
yo dream,
And we could move to L.A. like ain't that your
team,
Well if not, then it is now
And I'ma take you to the water + find a romantic
spot where we could sit down,
And I'ma breakdown bout how I'ma always be
down,
I'ma always make you smile, and I'ma always
make you laugh, and you gon' look at me, like,
Kassius you such a clown,
Now we holding hands kickin cans, toes in the sand,
band in the background while we ball dance,
So when we lock eyes, it'll be no surprise,
when you say to me gently Kash I'm so proud

EXPLORE

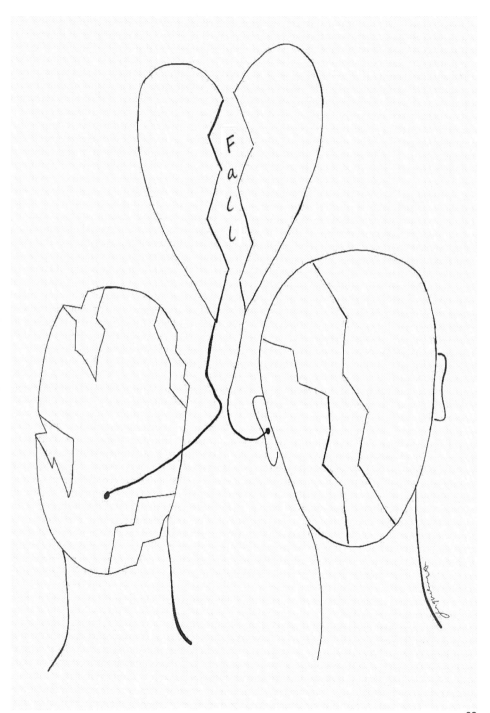

Pride

Man's greatest weakness
Some may not agree
But I've seen it time and time again
And not just in others
But frequently in me
The urgency to protect
This wall called ego
So admitting wrong
Was not in my vocabulary
I've fallen victim to this weakness
For I've lost so much
Trying to keep up with him
Friends gone because I wouldn't compromise
Partners lost in the distance
Because feelings
And wrongs
I never owned
Still a daily struggle
Trying to stand strong
And not prideful
So pray for me on this quest
To let go of my ego
Before I become the downfall
To my own hu-man

Dead Wrong

Blind sighted by all of society's rules
I've missed out on some of you
Time passed, opportunities missed
Only leaving you in the midst of drafts never
finished
If only I knew what I know now
Then I wouldn't of lost my way
Ignoring all the facts along the way
Always being the stray
Thinking that I'm superwoman
Invincible and strong never showing weakness
Any evidence of deterioration refuse to surface
Dragging you down in the fight
You were the victim in my life
Vulnerable
Flustered
Patient
It took some time to realize
That you are the oxygen that keeps me alive
Being selfish to the selfless
Hurting me as much as I did you
When all along we were just DEAD WRONG
It's you that I want in my life
It's you that I need by my side
You are the moon that lights up my night
When I hear your name I still get butterflies
As my heartbeat rises while staring into those
beautiful eyes
I love the way you sparkle up my life

Distant Lover

I thought it would be easy
Yes I said easy
I thought it would be easy
Loving you from a distance
But the more I try to create space
Your magnetic force keeps pulling me back
Back into your arms to hold
With that beating organ in our chests
Creating a sweet tune to my soul
I thought it would be easy
Loving you from a distance
But like the saying says
The distance grew my heart's desire for you
Only creating an acceleration
Of heartbeats when you were around
My heart became fearless
With the strength of the beats
In my chest
I thought it would be easy
Loving you from a distance
Usually I'm good with falling back
Lean in just enough to win you over
And when my heart gets restless
Ease my way into a seatbelt
But with you it was different
For once the unfamiliar
Feeling was one I wanted to stay
Continuing in "I love yous"
And romantic things
A tale I'd be telling if I told you
I'm not in too deep
So afraid to let you see that side of me
Composure is what I'm trying to keep
I thought it would be easy
Loving you from a distance
Looks like I'll have to tell that lie
to finish this story

Love you in the dark

In the dark is where we meet
but it is there that I can't love you

Waves spread wide as it clashes against my face
Hitting me hard with every lash
As I drift farther from your space
Backsliding like I'm on skates
Thinking to myself
remove your eyes off me so I can escape
I'm far too ashamed to do it with your eyes searching mine
Foolish to think that you won't see
As your being is compressed in my everything

Almost like everything that's supposed
to work in synch is somehow
drowning in the flood I've created
To believe that loving you in the dark would be easier
Bottled up emotions and stresses that I fail to express
Neglecting to connect to your cell tower
Instead making soft connections
to towers that don't stretch to you
Calls dropped
Communication lost
Mind continues to spin
Calls itself searching
Searching for light
Because your GOSPEL shines so bright
Trying to find a glimpse of hope you impregnated me with
Back when I was riding waves of love and light
Waves of trust and truth
Waves of peace and happiness
Waves of faith and hope
but most importantly waves of you

I can't love you in the dark
Feels like we're oceans apart

Say

What's on your mind
Before we run out of time
For once we cannot be shy
Must spit what's on our mind
For there is fear that we might
Fall all the way back
With everything unsaid
Bottled up hurt from overtime
Become so distant like a foreign land
So say what you have to say
I'd rather hear the pain
Than watch us fade away
And always sit around
With my thoughts of "what ifs"

Ignored

Message sent
No reply
Yet visions of you
Appear on my timeline
I get it
No strings attached
So I guess this is a punishment
For not spending the night
Got me in my feelings
And play the victim
Dub me as the villain
Cause that's the easy way out
IGNORED
Just like daddy would
Have me in the dark
With no sharing of feelings
Torture of always waiting
Looking for the glimpse of light
I guess it's time to retract
Rebuild these walls
I know how to construct
Can't handle daddy's
Mess twice
Check myself
Before I wreck myself
Block the feelings
Before memories turn to
Sour moments
Ouch ..
I should have
Learned from all the signs
Now I'm here
Being ignored
In my feelings
Like it wasn't partially my doing

Broken

Fragments of mistrust
And lust
Coupled together
With unseen devices
Creating me
But not that of a whole piece
More like fragments
Of puzzle pieces
Broken
Trying to fix the pieces
That mom and dad created
Broken
Fragments of miscommunication
So she stumbles on her words
Can't express her feelings
Hold everything
Until it's breaking SZN
Broken
Not even glue
Can keep the pieces together
But she has learned
Even the broken has an outlet
Someone to listen
To the words that hurt
Someone to catch
The overflow of tears
So for those broken
Just remember
Joy comes in the morning
Broken
Still makes for
Beautiful creations

Pain

Ouch,
I felt the dagger
Straight
To my side
I fell to my knees
To pray
But
It seemed
Like God
Had shunned me
Ouch
The dagger
Protruding out
Feelings spraying
Bleeding deep within
The pain felt
Unfamiliar
It was toxic
It was spiritual
I needed restoration
But I was
So caught in
His warped love
That when I fell
To my knees
God felt
Unfamiliar to me
I was so caught
In him
That my connection
Was weak
It was spiritual
It was pain
I never
Needed to feel

Promise

I promise..
The infamous words of a liar
The two words that separate you and me
The words you whispered when
you claimed you'd stay true
The words you made me eagerly believe
The words that you said after
everything would be alright
The words that you said after
you're the only one I want in my life
Those same two words you convinced my mother
That you were a son she could trust
The words that separates a man from a boy
I PROMISE
It was my fault for believing
you when you said it.
I promise that was the last time
I believed your lies

But

The word that comes
Before an excuse
The word I wish
I never knew
When it came to you
But
The segway to emotions
I'd rather not feel
Just one word
Has the power
To drop my heartbeat
But
Sometimes it lasts in love
But
Sometimes it hurts instead
But
If it's meant to be
It'll be
But
You'll grow through the pain
But
Let go and breathe
But
I never loved you
But
It's time to say goodbye
But
At least we tried
But
I hope you find
Someone that can make you happy
But
The segway to emotions
I'd rather not feel

Pillows

Pillows filled with tears
Unanswered questions seem to pierce her ears
One in the morning
And she can't seem to sleep
Episodes of fiction
Used to fill the void of what's lacking
Doesn't know the solution to her problem
So she continues to cry
OUT
To the only one she can reach
But in this moment even he seems too bleak
& distant like these miles between
Heaven and earth
Can't stop the tears from flowing
So she sits in her bed and writes poems
Hoping to close the gap she feels
Hoping to ease the pain before she sleeps
Hoping for better tomorrows and cheers
But deep down she hopes
That tomorrow won't be like yesterday
Covered in shame and guilt and questioning
Tomorrow she just hopes for eyes
that don't speak of tears and no sleep

Neglected

Or is it forgotten
Placed in the back of the wall
Plastered like a chameleon in disguise
So unnoticed
That I forget my presence
Been overlooked for so long
That the feeling of neglect
Feels like love
No time of quality
No open communication
Just microwave conversations
NEGLECTED
Like unshaved legs in the winter
No attention given
Lost in the journeys of life
Caught up in the tasks
Of tomorrow
In between hope and fear
Screaming for love
To fill the void
The dark hole
It's clear
That this abyss
Is her new
Definition of love
Neglected

Last night (again)

Last night
Was the last time I said goodbye
I wanted to be your friend
But you had other plans
You shut me out
And made me feel little
Took ME back to a memory
Of where daddy lacked
But I can't just blame you for this
Because I allowed myself
To drown
Choosing not to wear
A life vest
I allowed you to seep
Into my spirit
And penetrate my heart
I thought we were friends
Thought you'd be able to
Trust me during hard times
You're so complicated
You keep stumbling
On unhealed brokenness
You refuse to own
So this may be
The last time I try
I never wanted our love to die
But I think this
Will have to be goodbye
I need stability
Not surprise fireworks every night
I'll always love you
But after last night
I don't know
If I can look at you
With Love's eyes
Last night just happened to be
goodbye for the last time

Pieces

She laid broken into pieces
Trying to figure out the puzzle
Of the mess she helped create
Whispers in her ears
About all the past pains
She had inflicted
& about all the hearts she didn't claim

She laid broken into pieces
Like shattered glass on a wooden floor
Self inflicted cuts from the shatters of the past
Pieces of hims lodged in her heart
Creating paper cuts that bleed silently

She laid broken into pieces
Like the abstract painting on the wall
People walk past and stare
Trying to figure out the art
That the pain had cause

She laid broken
Fragmented
Portioned
Sectioned
into Pieces

I Can't Love You

I can't love you
Not because I don't want to
But because I'm hurting too
& you just want me because
You feel like I can fill that gap
Between those lonely nights & that uneasy feeling
But the truth is I can't love you
Because just like you I'm hurting too
Only thing is I've come to terms with my truth
But you didn't want to believe me
When I told you how it'd be
You thought it could be different
Thought you could change what I said it would be
But in reality it was just as I said
That my emotions were tied up in pain
Too cluttered to separate the pain from the love
So when you smiled bright, I didn't notice
When you tried, I barely noticed
When you opened up I didn't take advantage
& as cliche as it's going to sound
I just wanted you to know that it wasn't just you
It's been me too, I can't love you
Not because I don't want to
But because I'm hurting too
& we all know the saying to be true
Hurt people .. hurt people
So let me save you from the pain
Let you go so she can appreciate the frame of your smile
So she can sprinkle magic on your pain
So she can whisper sweet somethings in your ears
Because if you stay on this train
It only goes one way
With the last stop at heart break
So baby take my word cause it ain't a game
I can't love you
Not because I don't want to
But because I'm hurting too

Interlude -- #Quest

QUEST

Time is of the essence but not to most. Think of the quest it took to get from coast to coast OR to venture to 9:37, 8, 9, 10, 11, its definitly not been a slice of heaven.

The Quest can be a mess if you let it. We often times over look the blessings and what it took to get it or what it took to save "huh" we often forget it.

I am really at a stand still with my thoughts or maybe since birth this is how I've been taught. To keep feelings and emotions inside and keep it in stride, this was especially evident when my father died. I was only just a boy only 17 years old. The pain was unbarable seeing that transition unfold.

Its easy for people to say "God would not put more on you than you can bare" especially when they aint the ones wrestling the bear. As time passed I continued my quest and made due. They say time is of the essence and how it flew, as time marched on and as a man I grew. learning in this quest for laugh, live, love things cant always turn out in the order above maybe even not at all.

Honestly too much of my quest has been spent chasing those three assets that I have gone lacking in areas of mind, body, and soul but now I can see the light as clear as day let it never fade as it leads the way to that american dream that seems so far in front knowing that the definition of Quest is the search for something while I push forward to my higher calling as challenges keep coming.

Its been a long hard discouraging road this quest of mine in search for happiness this many will not find. Oh but I will indeed find that happy place, a place just right for me, and it will be called my space and in this space I will be able to reach back in last place to counsel, uplift, and encourage them as they run their race.   **EXPLORE** David Quest

Hello

Sweetness or misery
The beginning of every goodbye
The most innocent word
Hello
But even in hello you can find hell
A simple introduction
With the power to alter your world
Hello
The beginning of every goodbye

Shower Thoughts

Water drip from my head to toe
Thoughts flow
With the flow
Of water
Trickling down my body
Thoughts of 'what ifs'
And 'had it been for'
And 'maybe if I had'
Thoughts
Composed of maybes
And thoughts of me
Without you
And flashes of images
of you with her,
Running through
Our last argument
Replaying all the things
I wish I said
Thoughts
Plague my mind
During this shower time
Which should be solitude
But instead
It's filled with
Conversations with all versions of me
About how
We could have done
Things differently

A letter to you

Dear you,
I vowed to never lay ink to paper
To write emotions triggered
By the remnants of you
But for some odd reason
You always seem to resurface
In people I thought I knew
You know all the habits
I wish you'd take responsibility for
But even in your aged days
You hide behind those immature walls
Of that of a young teenage boy
I guess I'll forever write letters to you
Because so much of me got wrapped up in you
constantly comparing the men
In my life to the memory of you
Constantly unlearning my favorite parts of you
Constantly suppressing the feelings I wish I never
knew
I vowed to never lay ink to paper
To write emotions triggered
by the remnants of you
But for some reason
I always find myself
Bleeding ink in memory of you

White

White became the color
That came to mind
When I thought of you
Ghost, empty, muted
Of no hue
You became dull like an
Unsharpened knife
You became pale
like you had no life

every word out of your mouth
Was a hollow promise
Empty like the white spaces
Not filled with ink
Quick to disappear
When any test of love surfaced

You became unfamiliar
Slowly disappearing with every lie
Slowing dissolving into someone
I thought I knew

Ghosted & Ghostly
Two languages you spoke fluently
Your invisible being
Became your new identity
You began to fade away
& I slowly lost the image of me
the one that you cherished so intensely

WHITE
Became the color
that came to mind when I thought of you
Ghost, empty, muted
Of no hue
You became dull like an
Unsharpened knife
You became pale
like you had no life

Fraud

in the voices of my students
as they refer to someone that
has done them wrong,
will do them wrong, or
partnering with another to do them wrong.
they use it so jokingly,
not knowing the weight it carries.
& the more and more I heard them say it
the more and more I thought of you.
YOU...yes..YOU. You're a FRAUD.
you have done wrong,
you continue to do wrong, yet
front like you do no wrong.
the epitome of fraudulent.
you lie, cheat, and steal.
lies that kill the soul,
cheating that kills the heart,
& stealing that takes away trust & joy
but to you you've done nothing wrong.
continuous scolding but no lesson learned.
just another day in the life of a FRAUD.
sad part is you may not even know of
this scandalous role you currently possess
but nevertheless you continue life with an abyss.
one day when the FEDS catch up to you,
everything you lied about will come to light,
everyone you cheated will kick you to the curb,
every relationship you stole from will just be
another "What if"
then you'll realize that you've been a person
intended to deceive others,
no credibility
just a FRAUD

Naked

She walked around naked
But fully clothed
She didn't even realized that she was stripped
Of herself
Her identity she had lost
It was wrapped up in an IT
See ..she was caught in dysfunction
But to her it was normal
Because she had created a place
In her mind that her situation was normal
Exactly where it needed to be
So deep in this connection
That she created excuses
For her tragedy
Walked around like a zombie
Going through the motions
Although her spirit told her to leave
See ..she was wrapped up in an IT
and unfortunately she didn't see
The built up debris in her chest
She would rather lay four feet to a bed
While sacrificing her peace
She walked around naked
But fully clothed
He didn't take her garments
But he stripped her mentally

He saved me

he saved me
when I didn't know
I needed saving
he was a parasite
attracted to my warmth
he took from me,
my space, my energy
but I was too blind to see
that his parasite tendencies
was killing me slowly
I was his host
he needed me to survive
he evaded all my defenses
he took from me,
my space, my energy
but I was too tired to leave
he digested my love so freely
allowing him to take
advantage of my brokenness
he took from me,
my space, my energy
he was a parasite
he took my love
but I had grown so
accustomed to the lack of energy
that I allowed him to deteriorate me
he took from me,
my space, my energy
and when he was finished
he shed me like his dead skin
and moved on to the next victim
he saved me
when I didn't know
I needed saving

The Gap

Somewhere in between wanting to be here
and wanting to disappear
Still trying to figure out how I fit into this space
Of loving you and acting like I don't care
The Gap
Seeing your image come across my screen
Fills me with joy yet distaste
Of how you could up and dip with no remorse
Leaving me lifeless like a dead corpse
The Gap
In between love and hate
Where love always seems to win
Even in my moments of past pain
Only sweet joys always seem to surface
The Gap
Missing you like you've always been here
Building stories of nothings
Characters with characteristics that will never exist
True love I'll never experience
The Gap
The space that will always be between you and me
The space I'll keep filling with
how I think it ought to be
The space where fantasy will never meet reality
The space that a true relationship
between you and me will probably never be
The Gap
Somewhere between wanting to be here
and wanting to disappear
Still trying to figure out how I fit into this space
Of loving you and acting like I don't care

Worthy

What's that anyways
Being engulfed with bliss
Has always been a wish
Trying to connect
With someone that has been disconnected
Tried to keep hope alive
But wallowed in thoughts of fear
Knowing that fear is sin
and I'm saved
And you I forgive
For all you didn't claim
Making small progress
But still seems to lead to pain
So I might leave this here
A poem to describe you once again
Thought I'd never curse your name
But still can't grasp
How one person could be so selfish
Never taking responsibility
For what is his
King of manipulation
Stories filled with lies
Always one sided narratives
That defies
My definition of
A worthy child

Love Story

No more running
it hurts me to see you hurt and torn
and it seems like I'm always the one that does it to you
So if I'm to sacrifice my happiness for yours
that's what I'm willing to do
Trust when I say this is no white flag
just showing my love for you, I may come off passive
but know that it's with quiet aggression
I've never had to fight for someone before
so excuse the don't know how tone
Daddy left young so fighting he's never done
Example I've followed my whole life
and it's been the wrong one
Tripping over my mistakes looks like I'm the dumb one
To follow a fool like him got me on
thin thread hanging on for dear love
I always thought I didn't deserve love
the one that was supposed to be my first love
left me with a black heart, No red to see
just the debris of misplaced trust & regrets of young love
Bastard child I've been on the run
So used to pain I find more comfort in that than I do love
Rather bend my head and cry than
to admit to a love that's natural
I've never been this vulnerable like I am now
Getting ready for anyway the table turns
Our spirit intertwine
Faith in God has kept me planted to stay and fight
If it's not right then let him decide
I love you because we've always beat time
When I'm with you we're like fine wine
Missing years but still we shine
Every time I leave it's like we lost no time
Cause when I'm with you it's always like the first time
So if this is the last time
know that I'll love you until the end of time
Signed - a heart that's been blind

The last day

You know that day that you opened your eyes
And everything that you had is now gone
The day that you finally grasp the concept of living
But you look around and your joy is moving on
Yea that day that time seems to move slowly along
cause everyone that's been waiting for you has now drifted
Gone with no footprints in the sand
Gone with no new area code or address change
Gone with no map or directions
Gone ... gone with the wind. Cliché right..but
Now you're stuck trying to figure out the pieces
To the crazy puzzle you created
For years others tried to analyze this abstract painting
Now you're sitting there just as lost
as outsiders looking in
The pieces don't fit, The colors don't match
The objects are hidden
So now instead of a clear interpretation
You sit there puzzled, confused, dazed
Wondering, what if…
I left footprints in the sand
Or a map with directions at hand
I'd have all the pieces to understand
Its complexity, Its pure simplicity
The pieces that connected my prides and joys
The colors that screamed love and war
The objects that contributed to trial and error
But those are now just what ifs….??
Instead you're left with an unfinished picture
Opened to any interpretation
And you, Well you,
You're still sitting there puzzled, confused, dazed,
wondering
Now everything and everyone you could have had is GONE
With no intentions of looking back
Your pieces, colors, objects are still oblivious to you
Today is the last day
I cried that last cry

Time

TIME is precious
one of the few things you can't get back
And I know I've said this TIME and TIME again
but it's you that I can't let go
I know they say TIME heals all
so I'm patiently waiting
for the bruises to turn to scars
And I know you'd do better
if circumstances were different
or maybe it's just me hoping
that if things stayed the same
then TIME wouldn't have changed
Maybe if you never left
we wouldn't have to play catch up
so much TIME has been lost
it's hard to pick up where we left off
but I see you making improvement and progress
I waited all this TIME
I guess it wouldn't hurt to wait a little more
TIME flies and stand still
at the same TIME
when it comes to you
so if TIME never let us intertwine again
just know you'll always have a place in
my heart
my soul
my life.
Ps phucktime ..but I love you

Forgive me

Forgive me for all the times I said I loved you
Not because I 'lied,' it just wasn't the whole truth
See how could I truly love you
When I was struggling to love me
& by me I mean all the parts of me
The parts that only Jesus sees
So when I said I loved you , It wasn't a lie
But a representation of love that wasn't yet defined
Forgive me for all the times I said I loved you
Because I didn't know then
That love was bigger than a 4 letter word
That love was composed of actions, actions that support
Healing that I hadn't experienced
Trauma that I hadn't name
Fears that I hadn't conquered
You see love is the true expression of freedom
& when I said I loved you I wasn't free
I was in bondage, shackled by demons I couldn't see
So forgive me for all the times I said I loved you
Because really my heart wanted to
But there was built up debris
That settled from past relationships
That I was reluctant to see
So when I said I loved you
It was really just 4 letters coming from a place of debris
A love that was made up in
Things that weren't truly defined
Like how your smile reminded me of fine wine
& how your eyes looked at me
Those times you cried
So forgive me for all the times I said I loved you
Not because I 'lied'
It just wasn't the whole truth
Because I know now that we both deserved better
You a woman with a heart uncluttered
& me a king that is a man of valor
Forgive me for all the times I said I loved you

Growth

you were like an untapped treasure waiting to bloom
and I was here ready to release you from your cocoon
no I'm not God but when it came to you
it was as if his potential through me
unleashed the best parts of you
your treasure became defined
and I found myself pouring
and giving of myself to your growth
and to your strength
you were like an untapped treasure
hiding in the shadows of mistaken identity
trapped behind the walls
that society had perceived you to be
a man with so much potential that before me went unseen
but now I'm glad to see that you've tapped into the gold
that I pulled from you
the gold that you've had all along
but was afraid to unleash to the world
I'm glad to see that your treasure is being shared
that you've grown into the man I always knew you could be
it's funny how growth can push and pull
pushing people together
and pulling people apart
for us growth happened so unexpectedly
& instead of a pull we were pushed
into uncommon territory
forced to unlearn habits
forced to see milestones without me

Ha growth,
I see what you did,
Now the world can see the best parts of you and me
Unfortunately, not together, but separately

Spring

it was spring
and I was suppose to feel
the joys of blossoming flowers
and hear the sounds of birds chirping
but all I could remember
was the whiff of your scented cologne
as it was touched by the sun of spring
and the concerts and all the songs we sang
all I could remember was how the
break in the season
reminded me of the best
times we had
and how I wish it would fall back
to those moments of happiness and bliss
but instead it was spring
our relationship wasn't still blooming
instead we watch each other from afar
wondering how things could ever be this distant
and how the cold bricks of winter
managed to sneak into this season of life and
laughter
oh dear spring,
I normally like you
but for this time around
you're just a reminder of him
in his best days
and I'm reminded of how much
time we've missed
and how his lips use to feel as we kissed ..

ugh spring..I normally like you!

Interlude: #Hopeless-heart + #Am-I

#HOPELESS HEART 06/03/15

My love for you is a maze I don't know
how to get out of, my tears fall deep, my emotions
run deeper, the sweetest kiss I've ever known
but out of those sweet lips was sour
words that killed me so deep inside all I could
do is cry sometimes I think you're my angel
from up above, but my demon I wish I never
loved... am I the dummy knowing I should
have left so long ago blinded by this thing
called love kinda hopeless? no, because
your beautiful face made me smile, dark
days turn around, & had my love for you
locked down. -Deanna S.

#AM I?

am I crazy for loving you? am I crazy for
letting you make my heart bloom? like a
flower... It needs rain to live & for some
reason I thought I needed you but honestly
I was just a fool my heart was on fire searching
for the water of real love to come down.
my eyes poured so much ▓▓▓▓▓▓.
▓▓▓▓▓▓▓ from my tears all my
emotions do is drown in my confused
lost mind always down from your cheating
& lying go a.head & try to hit me if you're
able man you know that my relations
should stable sometime I know you thinking
Im not something you'safraid of cause you
think that you see what Im made of
but sadly you dont know the real me
the real "De" the person that gave you
there heart & the key ♡ so am I crazy
for loving you? am I crazy for letting you make my
heart bloom? **EXPLORE** -Deanna Sanders

Permission to Love

Sometimes our hearts cry
From pain we played a role in inflicting
It aches from the heartaches
Of trust broken
And condemnation
In our spirit
Not for someone else
But for us
We get trapped in the
Cycle of condemning ourselves
For mistakes made
And we reiterate
The words
"I deserved it"
We trap ourselves
In what happened
Instead of what could be
And we allow the enemy
To retell stories of brokenness
We forget to be honest
With us
And to own all the parts
That we caused
Just so that we can keep this facade of
Playing the victim
But I urge you to create
a moment to forgive yourself
Don't limit your possibilities
To feed the narratives
Of untrue stories
Of the love that you can give
This is a poem for you
A poem to give yourself
Permission to love
Not just YOU
But give yourself
Permission to love again

"Between what is said
And not meant and what
Is meant and not said;
MOST LOVE IS LOST"
                              - Khalil Gibran

Acknowledgements

First I want to thank God for always being
consistent and constant in all of my
seasons.

I want to say thank you to my tribe
which makes up the most dynamic family,
friends and youth a girl could ask for.
You guys are really special to me. You
never cease to encourage, support, and
inspire me. THANKS for being my hype men &
women, thanks for praying for and with me,
thanks for holding me down in every season
of love. Y'all are the real GOATS of my
life.

A special thanks to
Jackie for the seasons cover art,
Jaziah for photography,
Juan, Jordan, Deanna, and Daniel for their
interludes and
Sharika for the book description,
Your gifts made this book even more
special to me. I am glad I could share
this with you.

Lastly, I want to thank YOU! Thank you for
believing in me as an author, for being
brave enough to rehash these emotions,
brave enough to heal, brave enough to love
again. You are special, you are loved, and
I am thankful that I get to share this
with you.

I love you all,
-Rolanda.

Made in the USA
Columbia, SC
14 February 2020